The "Gender-Inclusive" Movement Among Churches of Christ

By
Kyle Pope

Truth Publications, Inc. • **CEI Bookstore**
220 S. Marion St. • Athens, Alabama 35611 • www.truthbooks.com

The "Gender-Inclusive" Movement
Among Churches of Christ

ISBN:10: 1-58427-381-X
ISBN: 13: 978-1-58427-381-3

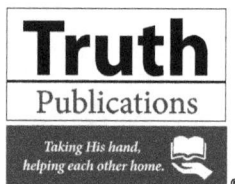

Truth
Publications

*Taking His hand,
helping each other home.*

Truth Publications, Inc.
CEI Bookstore
220 S. Marion St. • Athens, Alabama 35611
1-855-492-6657 • www.truthbooks.com

Contents

Preface

The topic of this study is not one that is well-known to many of our brethren. Among those who have insisted upon biblical authority for all doctrine and practice, gender issues have not been prominent causes of discussion or conflict. Students of translation may hear the term "gender-inclusive" and think we are considering whether to translate masculine terms like "mankind" with more generic terms like "humanity." In this application of the term, "gender-inclusive" advocates in the religious world have moved biblical translators to reject male pronouns applied to God and other indications of male leadership in the home and church in their paraphrases of Scripture. This is not the focus of this study. Instead we are considering a growing movement among mainstream churches of Christ to *include* women in roles of leadership and public teaching. Its advocates identify themselves as "gender-inclusive," because of their view that women have been *excluded* from these roles. Although I use this term in the title of this study I take exception to it, and reject the premise that underlies its use. Simply because God has assigned different roles to different genders does not infer that any gender has been *excluded*. I offer this study in the hopes that it may help us guard against the rise of this heresy. If history is any indication what begins in the mainstream doesn't take long to creep in even among those who were once the most conservative. May we prepare ourselves to face this emotional and culturally explosive issue with love, courage, and a fervent love for God and His word.

Kyle Pope
kmpope@att.net

5

Introduction

A quiet but volatile movement is starting to brew within congregations that still identify themselves as "churches of Christ." Historically, in America those who have called themselves "churches of Christ" have sought to reject denominational practices, teachings, and organization not found within God's word. In the mid-twentieth century many churches began to abandon this objective when they accepted social practices, evangelistic schemes, and church support of human institutions with no scriptural authority. This same spirit is now manifesting itself in yet another move towards ideas long ago adopted by the religious world. A website known as *Where the Spirit Leads,* maintained by a man named Wiley Clarkson, articulates the objectives of this movement. Advocating what he calls "Gender Equality and Inclusivity in the Churches of Christ," Clarkson maintains a listing of congregations he identifies as "Gender Inclusive Churches of Christ." In order to be included on his list, five criteria must be met:

Listings are now being compiled of congregations identified as "gender-inclusive."

1. Does this church use women in the worship to help lead worship by leading prayer, giving communion talks, leading singing, etc.?

The "Gender-Inclusive" Movement
Among Churches of Christ

2. Are women used to their fullest capabilities to teach all age groups regardless of gender in Bible classes?
3. Do women serve in leadership positions such as pulpit minister, worship leader, deacon, and elder?
4. Does the church publish a clear statement of purpose to be an egalitarian church or gender inclusive church on their web site?
5. Is a woman serving only in the position of Children's Minister or Women's Minister and none of the above apply?[1]

Clarkson posts articles and links advocating this position, some of which are drawn from CBE International ("Christians for Biblical Equality") a non-profit organization among denominational churches listing criteria similar to Clarkson's. While his listing as of January 2012 had only 26 congregations, by June it had grown to 41 in the US and 2 in Canada![2] Clarkson himself predicts, "the issue of women's roles in the teaching, worship, ministry, and leadership of the Churches of Christ...will be the single most discussed and divisive issue in the first few years of the 21st century."[3] I fear his prediction may have more validity than many of us have previously recognized. In this study we will survey some of the basic objectives of this movement and analyze the biblical teachings that address these issues.

---

[1] January 11, 2012 update, http://www.clarksons.org/spiritleads/gender_inclusive_churches.htm.

[2] June 25, 2012 update, http://www.wherethespiritleads.org/gender_inclusive_churches.htm.

[3] "Focusing on the Questions – Finding the Answers!" http://www.clarksons.org/spiritleads/spiritleads.htm.

What Is The Issue?

A fundamental premise advanced by advocates of this movement is that women within churches of Christ have been neglected and discriminated against by a male dominated leadership unwilling to allow their sisters in Christ to use the gifts that God has given them. Floyd E. Rose, in an e-book that Clarkson posts on his website entitled *An Idea Whose Time Has Come*, repeatedly compares the treatment of women within the church to slavery or racism. He claims, "to deny women, because of their gender, the right to do whatever God has given them the ability and desire to do is wrong, just as it was wrong to deny Afri-

If "all are one in Christ" must gender roles be abandoned?

can-Americans the right to do what God had given them the ability and desire to do based on race" (16). The primary biblical text that is offered in defense of their position is Galatians 3:28, where Paul through the Holy Spirit asserts boldly that in Christ, **"There is neither Jew nor Greek, there is neither slave nor free, there is neither male nor female; for you are all one in Christ Jesus"** (NKJV). If "all are one," and race, gender, and servitude are nothing, it is argued that all roles of leadership, service, and teaching must be shared.

9

The "Gender-Inclusive" Movement
Among Churches of Christ

What Must Determine Our Practice?

Any student of religious history must recognize that to defend or reject a doctrine on the basis of what has been done in the past is a dangerous practice. Human beings have often done the right thing in an improper way, or accepted sinful innovations in an attempt to advance a legitimate concern. It is not about what mankind has done in the past but what God has authorized through His word. If, as the Holy Spirit asserts, Scripture provides to us what is needed, **"that the man of God may be complete, thoroughly equipped for every good work"** (2 Tim. 3:16-17), we must be willing to follow its dictates in the confidence that it is God's will regarding our behavior. When Scripture limits our behavior, we must resist the impulse to choose *what feels right to us*—**"It is not in man who walks to direct his own steps"** (Jer. 10:23). The drunkard may wish that God had not commanded him to **"be sober"** (1 Pet. 5:8), but he must not argue that God's command is no longer applicable today. The homosexual may feel strongly that what he feels inclined to do, must be acceptable before God, but he must not rationalize away God's prohibition of this behavior by claiming *it's been mistranslated* (1 Cor. 6:9). There may have been ways in which the authorized liberties of Christian women have been unduly limited in the past. However, to resolve this error we must not ignore or rationalize away the clear teaching of Scripture in order to correct a perceived injustice.

Equality in Christ

Under Christ there has always been *equality* in terms of the value, worth, importance, love, concern, and relationship that God has with His children. Galatians 3:28 follows the powerful asser-

The "Gender-Inclusive" Movement
Among Churches of Christ

tion of how this relationship comes about. **"Through faith"** we may become **"sons of God"** (Gal. 3:26) when we **"put on Christ"** by being **"baptized into Christ"** (Gal. 3:27). Having done so, we are considered **"Abraham's seed"** and **"heirs according to the promise"** (Gal. 3:29). Equality of relationship, however, does not mean that we all have the same responsibilities or roles. As a Christian, I am just as valuable before God as any one of the twelve apostles, but I absolutely have not been entrusted with the unique responsibility and role these men held. They were promised that God would directly give them words to say (Matt. 13:11), guide them into the complete revelation of God's word establishing the New Covenant (John 16:13). This granted to them the special role of acting as a **"foundation"** of the church of which Jesus Christ is the **"Chief cornerstone"** (Eph. 2:20). Was that partiality on the part of God? Have I been excluded or discriminated against in this? No! Just as in the Parable of the

> In Christ every soul is as valuable to God as every other, but not all share the same work.

Talents, God has the right to assign different works to His servants as He sees fit (cf. Matt. 25:14-30). In the church, every soul is just as valuable to God in Christ as every other soul, however, not every Christian is to be considered one of the group of leaders over a local congregation known as "elders." There are specific qualifications that the Holy Spirit has set down which such leaders must meet (cf. 1 Tim. 3:1-7; Titus 1:5-9). If I do not possess some of these qualifications am I a *second-class citizen* before God? No. Am I of less value before God? No. I simply have other responsibilities that I must meet in humility and submission.

The "Gender-Inclusive" Movement
Among Churches of Christ

In the next chapter we will note that some of the areas in which the Lord has set limitations on women's responsibilities and roles have nothing to do with discrimination, inequality, or value, but as in the above examples are simply a reflection of God's distribution of different assignments to different servants of equal value before Him.

Study Questions

1. What positions of leadership in the local church do advocates of the "Gender-Inlclusive" Movement seek to attain for women?
2. What is CBE International?
3. How do advocates of this movement argue that Galatians 3:28 should be applied?
4. What are some problems with appealing to the past in order to determine practice in the church?
5. What should determine practice in the church?
6. What are some ways that equality in Christ does not mean that all responsibilities must be shared?

Restrictions and Their Context

As this issue is discussed it is often treated as if any restrictions regarding these matters came from the mind of man and his desire to *subjugate* women. Edward Fudge, for example writes, "I believe that we have allowed a male-dominated culture of the past several centuries to shape our thinking and cause us unknowingly to misread and misapply the two passages of Scripture which might sound like they prohibit the public exercise by women of speaking gifts (1 Cor. 14:34-35 and 1 Tim. 2:12)."[1] Certainly, human beings can *misread* and *misapply* Scripture, but we must remember it is the Holy Spirit that led Paul to write these things. I fear that it is our own failure to properly discern the nature and the context of the commands of these "two Scriptures" that has contributed to the confusion which now exists, and the unscriptural reaction to this confusion demonstrated by the "Gender-Inclusive" Movement.

> **Have we properly discerned the nature and context of these texts?**

Properly we must acknowledge that there are far more than just "two Scriptures" that outline principles concerning submission and the restriction of women's roles within the church, yet for our purposes let's focus on three noted in the chart on the next page:

---

[1] "Women Teaching Men" http://www.wherethespiritleads.org/spiritleads/women_teaching_men.htm.

The "Gender-Inclusive" Movement
Among Churches of Christ

Women's Restrictions in the New Testament and Their Context

1 Corinthians 14:34-35	1 Timothy 2:11-12	Acts 18:24-26
Context: Spiritual gifts and conduct in the assembly of the church.	**Context:** General conduct— not specifically the assembly of the church.	**Context:** A private meeting outside of an assembly of the church.
Command: "Keep silent"	**Command:** Learn in "quietness" (ASV) or "quietly" (NASB).	**Example:** "They took him aside" and (in the Greek) "they explained to him the way of God more accurately."
Prohibition: A woman is not permitted to speak when the congregation is assembled as a church.	**Prohibition:** In general conduct a woman may not teach or exercise authority over a man.	**Necessary Inference:** In a setting outside of the assembly of the church (such as a Bible class) a woman may discuss spiritual things with those other than her husband, while maintaining a submissive and quiet disposition.

Let's start with the least restrictive and work our way towards the most restrictive.

Acts 18:24-26: This text records the efforts of two Christians, a husband and wife named Aquila and Priscilla, to teach a man named Apollos. Apollos was a Jewish teacher who knew only the **"baptism of John"** (Acts 18:25), but was said to have been "eloquent" and "mighty in the Scriptures" (Acts 18:24). He taught in the synagogue in Ephesus, and Aquila and Priscilla heard him there (Acts 18:26a). The text says, **"they took him aside and explained to him the way of God more accurately"** (Acts 18:26b, NKJV). The word translated "they took...aside" in Greek is *proselabonto* (προσελάβοντο). In Greek (unlike English) endings are attached onto the verb that indicate who carries out the action of the verb. In this case, for example, the *-nto* ending indicates that "they" did this. If it had ended with simply *-to* it would indicate that "he" (that is Aquila) did it alone. We note that this did not happen in a church assembly or even as Apollos spoke in the synagogue, but rather "they took him aside."

In the same way, the word translated **"explained"** is *exethento* (ἐξέθεντο). We notice that it also has the *-nto* ending, which also indicates that "*they* explained" these things to Apollos. In other words Priscilla also helped Apollos understand the gospel. So, is it wrong for a woman to discuss spiritual things with a man other than her husband? No. In a context outside of the assembly of the church, Priscilla helped to explain the truth of the gospel to Apollos. Did she *lead* this discussion? Not if we are to harmonize this account with Paul's teaching in our next text...

> A woman can discuss spiritual things with men outside of the assembly of the church.

1 Timothy 2:11-12: This text comes as Paul teaches the young preacher Timothy about a variety of different things related to proper Christian conduct. Its context is general. Four verses before Paul gives commands for men **"everywhere"** (1 Tim. 2:8). Immediately before our text Paul teaches women to **"adorn themselves with modest apparel"** (1 Tim. 2:9)—an instruction that clearly pertains to a woman's general conduct in public settings "everywhere." Paul then moves from modesty to command: **"Let a woman learn in quietness with all subjection. But I permit not a woman to teach, nor to have dominion over a man, but to be in quietness"** (1 Tim. 2:11-12, ASV). Edward Fudge, tries to argue, "In making this strange statement, the apostle was undoubtedly correcting some specific misbehavior at Ephesus."[2] There is nothing in the text to indicate this! In fact, in the next verses Paul appeals to the order of Adam and Eve's sin in the garden as explanation of the reason for this rule (1 Tim. 2:13-15). The consequences of their sin are universal (cf. Gen. 3:16-19). We must remember, in our text that the closest indication before this of the scope of Paul's command is the reference to men "everywhere" (1 Tim. 2:8). That indicates this is a general command, not merely a specific solution to a specific problem.

In this text, what does Paul *command* and what does he *prohibit?* In both verses Paul used the word *hēsuchia* (ἡσυχία) translated "quietness." Thayer explains that it describes the lifestyle, "of one who stays at home doing his own work, and does not officiously meddle with the affairs of others." This is not referring to absolute silence but a quiet disposition. At all times, a woman is to

> A woman must maintain a quiet disposition at all times.

have a quiet disposition. Proverbs 7:10-11 describes the antithesis of this in the woman with "the attire of a harlot" who is **"loud and rebellious"** and unwilling to **"stay at home"** (NKJV). Paul forbids a woman **"to teach or to have authority over a man"** (1 Tim. 2:12). Our non-class brethren have argued from this text that a woman can *never* teach in a formal class setting, however, Paul told Titus that women are to be **"teachers of good things"** (Titus 2:3), who **"admonish the young women"** how to behave

[2] "Women Teaching Men" http://www.wherethespiritleads.org/spiritleads/women_teaching_men.htm.

The "Gender-Inclusive" Movement
Among Churches of Christ

(Titus 2:4). As a child, Timothy apparently learned Scripture from his mother and grandmother, since his father was a Greek (2 Tim. 1:5; cf. 3:15; Acts 16:1). Paul commends this.

The issue doesn't seem to be the formality of the teaching but rather the role and exercise of authority. Women may teach children and other women, but they may not **"have dominion"** (ASV) or **"have authority"** (NKJV) over a man. This infers a religious context, as Scripture does not condemn royal or political authority held by a woman (cf. Acts 8:27). Does that mean an adult man can never learn something from a woman? No. As in the example of Aquila and Priscilla **"they explained to him the way of God more accurately"** (Acts 18:26), but we can infer that Priscilla did so with a quiet disposition in full submission to her husband. She did not *lead* the study. Does this mean that a woman could teach in the assembly of the church so long as she is in submission to her husband? Not if she is to be obedient to the next text we will consider from the chart above in our next chapter.

Study Questions

1. How can we know that Priscilla also explained the gospel to Apollos? Was this in a church assembly?
2. What are some indications that 1 Timothy 2:11-12 is talking about general conduct, not the assembly?
3. What does it mean to "have dominion" or "authority" over someone else?

First Corinthians 14:34-35

In the previous chapter we began consideration of three texts that outline the role and restrictions of women in the New Testament, as seen in the chart below:

Women's Restrictions in the New Testament and Their Context

1 Corinthians 14:34-35	1 Timothy 2:11-12	Acts 18:24-26
Context: Spiritual gifts and conduct in the assembly of the church.	**Context:** General conduct— not specifically the assembly of the church.	**Context:** A private meeting outside of an assembly of the church.
Command: "Keep silent"	**Command:** Learn in "quietness" (ASV) or "quietly" (NASB).	**Example:** "They took him aside" and (in the Greek) "they explained to him the way of God more accurately."
Prohibition: A woman is not permitted to speak when the congregation is assembled as a church.	**Prohibition:** In general conduct a woman may not teach or exercise authority over a man.	**Necessary Inference:** In a setting outside of the assembly of the church (such as a Bible class) a woman may discuss spiritual things with those other than her husband, while maintaining a submissive and quiet disposition.

We learned from Acts 18:24-26 that a woman is authorized to discuss spiritual matters with men in settings outside of the assembly, although she must still maintain a quiet and submissive disposition. We learned from 1 Timothy 2:11-12, that a woman is

The "Gender-Inclusive" Movement
Among Churches of Christ

not to teach or exercise authority over a man in religious matters. A woman may teach children and other women (Titus 2:3-4; 2 Tim. 1:5; cf. 3:15; Acts 16:1), but according to Scripture she is not permitted to lead a class over a man. Her influence to teach a man (as in the case of Apollos) must involve submission. We now consider the most restrictive text regarding this matter...

1 Corinthians 14:34-35: The context of this text comes in a broad section that began in chapter eleven and spans through chapter fourteen. Paul first addressed some general principles regarding the demonstration of female submission to men (1 Cor. 11:1-16), then slowly narrows the context to **"when you come together as a church"** (1 Cor. 11:18). In this context Paul first addressed the Lord's Supper (1 Cor. 11:17-34) and then moved to the use of spiritual gifts in the assembly (1 Cor. 12:1-14:40). The context is undeniable—it is behavior **"in the church"** (1 Cor,. 11:18, 22; 12:28; 14:4, 5, 12, 19, 23, 28, 35). We should note that women are

> The context of this text is clear—it is "in the church."

not the only ones restricted within this context. One who could speak in a foreign tongue was to **"keep silent"** (1 Cor. 14:28) if there was no interpreter. Even the prophet, to whom something was revealed during the assembly was to **"keep silent"** (1 Cor. 14:30) until another prophet finished speaking. While miraculous spiritual gifts have passed away (cf. 1 Cor. 13:8-12), this passage teaches many principles regarding conduct in church assemblies in any age. For example, Paul concludes this section with the admonition, **"let all things be done decently and in order"** (1 Cor. 14:40). Assemblies of the church are not to be chaotic and disorganized, but reverent, orderly, and suited for worship and edification.

The "Gender-Inclusive" Movement
Among Churches of Christ

It is within this context that the Holy Spirit leads Paul to command: **"Let your women keep silent in the churches, for they
are not permitted to speak; but they are to be submissive, as
the law also says. And if they want to learn something, let
them ask their own husbands at home; for it is shameful for
women to speak in church"** (1 Cor. 14:34-35). A simple reading
of this text should settle the whole matter. Paul declares through
the Holy Spirit that a woman may not "speak in church" and to do
so is "shameful." This is not Paul's opinion or personal prefer-
ence. Only two verses after this he declared, **"the things which I
write to you are the commandments of the Lord"** (1 Cor. 14:37).
This is not talking about general behavior. A woman is not to be
silent at all times. Rather, in the specific context of the local church
assembled a woman is to "be silent."

Challenges to this Position

Unfortunately, for advocates of the "Gender-Inclusive" movement, simple and clear truth is not enough to answer this issue.
Lance Pape, former "co-minister" with his wife Katie Hayes of
West Islip Church of Christ on Long Island New York, adminis-
ters a website called *Gender Justice and Churches of Christ*
(www.gal328.org). In answering the challenges posed by 1 Timothy 2:11-15 and 1 Corinthians 14:33b-36 he argues that understanding these texts calls for "interpretive humility, and a sensi-
tivity to the theological undercurrents in Scripture" going on to
offer Galatians 3 and Acts 15 as "good starting points for thinking theologically about gender" arguing that "1 Corinthians 14
and 1 Timothy 2 do not."[1] This is a puzzling statement. We noted

---

[1] "Frequently Raised Objections 5." http://www.gal328.org/articles/Pape-
FRO.html#five.

The "Gender-Inclusive" Movement
Among Churches of Christ

in our first chapter the prominent use of Galatians 3:28 by advocates of this position because of its teaching that in Christ **"there is neither male nor female for you are all one in Christ Jesus"** (NKJV). Yet, we also noted that equality of value does not mean equality of responsibility and role (cf. the apostles vs. all Christians). Pape's appeal to Acts 15 is curious. This text says nothing about gender, but addresses the controversy over the circumcision of Gentile converts. Undoubtedly, Pape is trying to compare Jewish and Gentile equality to male and female equality, but the difference is we have no Scripture restricting Gentile roles and responsibilities. Whatever our "starting point" we must still accept all of Scripture for what it says. I would agree that we must approach Scripture with "humility" but this is not accomplished by rejecting what a text says but by carefully harmonizing Scripture with Scripture so that we may *rightly divide* the word (2 Tim. 2:15).

When the local church is assembled "as a church" a woman is to keep silent.

Edward Fudge addresses our text more directly, but tries to argue that this is addressing "some disorderly women who apparently are interrupting the proceedings with their questions," going on to argue that the passage "certainly is still authoritative" but applies specifically to those who would begin to "call out" in the assembly while someone else is speaking.[2] This interpreta-

---

[2] "Women 'Be Silent' in the Chruch (1)." http://wherethespiritleads.org/spirit-leads/Women%20Be%20Silent.htm.

tion may confuse the prohibitions to the tongue speaker (14:28) and the prophet (14:30) with what is commanded regarding women (14:34-35). It is unclear whether women at Corinth had actually begun to speak, or if Paul was simply laying down the governing ordinance regarding possible behavior. In either case, Paul offers the binding command **"Let your women keep silent in the churches"** (14:34). Can we read this and conclude "so long as women behave orderly they *can speak?"* No. That is the same mistake our liberal brethren make in 1 Corinthians 11:17-34. There we have a PROBLEM—the Corinthians had abused the Lord's Supper making it a common meal (11:21-22). We also have a CORRECTION—the Lord's Supper was intended as a memorial (11:23-26). But the Holy Spirit also offers the SOLUTION—eat at home for hunger (11:34). Social meals are not the business of the church.

In our text, if we try to say there was a PROBLEM—women were perhaps speaking out in a disorderly manner, what is the CORRECTION and SOLUTION? Clearly the CORRECTION is, **"…it is shameful for a woman to speak in church."** If this were to happen it is not proper behavior. But the SOLUTION is also clear, **"…if they want to learn something, let them ask their own husbands at home."** This is in perfect harmony with Acts 18:24-26 and 1 Timothy 2:11-12—in a context outside of the church assembly a woman may discuss spiritual matters. That doesn't say "so long as she behaves orderly she can speak" or

> When the Lord identifies something as "shameful" how can we treat it as acceptable?

even "so long as she doesn't teach she can speak"—it prohibits a woman from speaking in the assembly of the church. In our next chapter we will consider some specific questions that this raises.

Study Questions

1. What is different about the context and prohibition in 1 Corinthians 14:34-35 and 1 Timothy 2:11-12?
2. Who is also commanded to "keep silent" in 1 Corinthians 14? Is this to be absolute silence?
3. How do advocates of the "Gender-Inclusive" Movement argue that Galatians 3 and Acts 15 apply to these questions? What is the flaw in this argument?
4. Does Paul's command in 1 Corinthians 14:34-35 prove that women *had* spoken in the assembly in Corinth?
5. How does this relate to the question of eating together as a church?

Questions

A key passage that challenges the objectives of the so-called "Gender-Inclusive" movement is First Corinthians 14:34-35. To understand how this applies to this issue we must consider some specific questions…

What Does this Command and What Does it Prohibit?

The Holy Spirit leads Paul to begin this text with the command **"let your women keep silent in the churches"** (NKJV). Unlike the word used in 1 Timothy 2:11-12 which properly applies to a quiet disposition the word *sigaō* (σιγάω) used here is much stronger. It is in the imperative form which indicates it is a command— **"women must be quiet"** (*Simple English New Testament*). The nine instances of the use of this word in the New Testament clearly demonstrate its force. It is used of the disciples' silence after God spoke from heaven (Luke 9:36); the crowd's silence after Jesus' answer about payment of taxes (Luke 20:26); of assemblies remaining silent to listen to a speaker (Acts 12:17; 15:12, 13); of the silence of God in concealing the mystery of the gospel in ages past (Rom. 16:25), and twice earlier in this very chapter of the tongue-speaker (1 Cor. 14:28) and the prophet (1 Cor. 14:30) who must remain silent if there was no interpreter or when another was speaking. This is absolute silence, not merely a quiet disposition.

To this command Paul further adds a prohibition, **"for they are not permitted to speak"** explaining further in the next verse **"it is shameful for a woman to·speak in church."** The word

The "Gender-Inclusive" Movement
Among Churches of Christ

laleō (λαλέω) translated **"to speak"** in both verses is a very broad word for oral communication. Thayer defines it "to utter a voice or emit a sound." It is used almost 300 times in the New Testament and 24 times in this chapter. Although it can be used of public speaking (1 Cor. 14:19), it is also applied to private conversations (John 4:26), or even to one speaking **"to himself, and to God"** (1 Cor. 14:28). The fact that Paul adds this prohibition is important. Unlike the command to the tongue-speaker (14:28) and prophet (14:30) who were to remain silent under specific conditions (i.e. no interpreter, or when another was speaking) this prohibition defines the terms under which a woman must remain silent—**"in the churches."** A woman is prohibited from speaking when the church is assembled as a church. This is not merely leading the congregation, but speaking out at all. This prohibition is more restrictive than the command to the tongue-speaker and prophet. To advocate a position that places women in the assembly of the church preaching, leading the worship, or even offering comments is a violation of this text. Another question, however, arises from this text...

> The type of speech is not specified—speaking "in the church" is simply prohibited.

What Does Paul Mean By "As The Law Also Says"?

Some see the command "to be submissive" as the connection Paul makes to the Law. Brother Mike Willis in his commentary on First Corinthians writes, "The reference to the law appears to be to Genesis 3:16. 'Unto the woman he said, "...thy desire shall be to thy husband and *he shall rule over thee*'"" (421, emphasis

25

MW). If Willis is correct, this parallels 1 Timothy 2:11-14 where Paul commands women to learn **"in quietness with all subjection"** (2:11, ASV). As we noted in chapter two, immediately after this command Paul offered Adam's creation before Eve (2:13) and Eve's sin (2:14) as the reason for male headship.

While Genesis 3:16 does show the principle of subjection, it does not illustrate that women were not permitted to speak **"in the churches."** I submit that the explanation may be found elsewhere. In the Hebrew Old Testament there were two words that referred to the "congregation" of Israel—*qahal* (קָהָל) and *'edah* (עֵדָה). Most of the time these words were used synonymously, but occasionally the word *qahal* had a special meaning. There were certain foreigners and even Israelites who could be considered a part of the Israelite community in a general sense but were prohibited from *entering* the *qahal* (Deut. 23:2). Jack P. Lewis, the respected language scholar among liberal brethren, calls this sense of *qahal* the congregation as a "judicial representative of the community" (*Theological Wordbook of the Old Testament,* II:790). This was not just any assembly of Israel, but a special assembly of the Israelites for worship and important purposes (cf. Deut. 4:10; Judg. 20:2; 1 Sam. 17:47; 2 Chron. 1:5).

> **Descriptions of the Israelite assembly illustrate principles regarding the church.**

How does this relate to our study? When the Greek translation of the Old Testament produced before the time of Christ translated *qahal* it generally used the Greek word *ekklēsia* (ἐκκλησία), rendered "church" in the New Testament. A study of both the Hebrew and Greek Old Testaments reveals that a woman never spoke before that portion of the Israelite community called the *qahal* or the *ekklesia*.[1] Paul's phrase, **"as the law also says"** may refer to this fact in that it precisely parallels what is taught in First Corinthians 14:34-35, women were silent in the *qahal* (i.e. *ekklesia* or "church").

When Are We "In the Church"?

When one is obedient to the gospel the Lord adds him or her to the church (Acts 2:47 KJV, NKJV). Because of this **"all the saints"** in a local congregation (Phil. 1:1) are considered part of the "church" in that place (cf. Phil. 4:15). Yet, it is clear that while one can be *in the church* as a member of the Lord's church (universally or locally) that does not mean that he or she is always assembled "in the church." This is clear in several passages. Jesus commanded in Matthew 18:17 after two or three call a sinner to repentance, **"if he refuses to hear them, tell it to the church. But if he refuses even to hear the church, let him be to you like a heathen and a tax collector."** Obviously we can only *tell* the "church" something when the church is assembled. Paul instructed that his epistle to the Colossians was to be read **"in the church of the Laodiceans"** (Col. 4:16). He is not talking about a building, but the assembly of the church. Paul rebuked the Corinthians for having divisions among them **"when you come together as a** [lit. 'in the'] **church"** (1 Cor. 11:18). The one who could speak in tongues was to be silent "in church" if there was no in-

---

[1] This is even true in the account of the daughters of Zelophehad, whose father died in the rebellion of Korah. They appeal for help before "all the congregation"—i.e. the *'edah* (Num. 27:2), an informal assembly of Israel, but they did not address the *qahal* or *ekklesia*.

terpreter (1 Cor. 14:28). The prohibition of 1 Corinthians 14:34-35 is talking about a restriction when a local church is assembled as a church. This is when one is "in the church."

So what determines when a group of Christians that are members of a local congregation are assembled "in the church" and when they are assembled for some other purpose? It is not merely being together, nor is it the nature of the activity. Every member of a local congregation could go fishing, shopping, engage in business together, or sing and study together, but that wouldn't mean they were fishing, shopping, doing business, or even necessarily studying as a church. The Old Testament may help us with this. How did the Israelites distinguish the more general assembly of Israel (the *'edah*) from the special representative assembly (called the *qahal*)? Numbers 10:1-7 outlined the procedure by which two silver trumpets were to be used to call the Israelites to meet or advance for various purposes. When both trumpets were blown, **"all the congregation (*'edah*) shall gather before you at the door of the tabernacle of meeting"** (10:3). However, there was some type of distinct call that summoned the *qahal*. Numbers 10:7 declared, **"When convening the assembly (*qahal*), however, you shall blow without sounding an alarm"** (NASB). So the same people could assemble for distinct purposes under which different rules would apply.

> We must make it clear when we are assembled "as a church" and when we are not.

The New Testament does not teach a method like sounding a trumpet to indicate when we are assembled for a different purpose, but the same principle may provide the answer. There must be a clear stated purpose that determines the reason for the assembly. Are the members assembled to go fishing?—Then they are not assembled "in the church." Are the members assembled for a Bible study that does not constitute the church assembled?—If this is clearly stated, although a woman cannot teach over a man, a women may discuss spiritual things with a submissive quiet disposition (Acts 18:24-26; 1 Tim. 2:11-12). If the members are assembled for the stated purpose of coming together "as a church" (cf. 1 Cor. 11:18) a woman must remain silent during the assembly of the church.

Are We Encouraging Violation of this Command?

While most congregations have rejected the more extreme violations of this command, I wonder if we aren't beginning to allow some small moves that actually encourage the violation of this injunction. For example, when a congregation assembles it is common for announcements to be made regarding the work of the church. We have already seen that it is possible for the members of a congregation to all be together and not be assembled "as a church," but is that the situation when announcements are made? In Jesus' teaching on church discipline He shows us that the announcement of church business is something that is done when the church is assembled—He commands to **"tell it to the church"** (Matt. 18:17). Even so, during the announcements the man making announcements may ask a woman something to clarify an announcement. How is this not speaking "in the church"? Another example might be responsive statements. I might greet the congregation in such a way that I am calling upon the congregation to respond with "good morning" or "good evening." In doing this am I not calling upon women to speak "in the church"? These may seem like small things, and certainly there is judgment that

The "Gender-Inclusive" Movement
Among Churches of Christ

comes into play in these things, but I fear that we may be opening the door to some habits that will be very hard reverse. In our last chapters we will address some final issues raised by the so-called "gender-inclusive" movement.

Study Questions

1. Does the word *sigao* merely refer to a quiet disposition or to absolute silence?
2. Does the word *laleo*, translated "speak" only refer to teaching? How is it used elsewhere?
3. What is the distinction between the Hebrew words *qahal* and *'edah*? Which word corresponds to the Greek word *ekklesia*, translated "church"?
4. In the Old Testament how did Israelites distinguish between the two types of assemblies?
5. When is a Christian "in the church" in the sense described in 1 Corinthians 14:34-35?

Women Deacons and Elders

In 2010 Dr. Stephen Johnson, and Dr. Lynette Sharp Penya of Abilene Christian University conducted a research project entitled "Gender Inclusivity in Church of Christ Congregations."[1] The project surveyed 45 congregations that demonstrated elements of "gender inclusivity" regarding their frequency of women's participation in 15 different "public religious activities." In spite of what we have seen in the previous chapters regarding the biblical prohibition of women speaking in the church assembly (1 Cor. 14:34-35) or teaching over a man (1 Tim. 2:11-12), Johnson and Penya found that 97.7% allowed women to read Scripture; 88.6% allowed women to teach adult classes with adult males present; 77.3% allowed women to lead prayer; 56.8% allowed women to lead singing; 20.5% allowed women to preach on Sunday morning or Wednesday night (6).

Research shows that a growing number of congregations are accepting these views.

Johnson and Penya also surveyed these congregations regarding leadership and "formal titles." While they found that

---

[1] "Gender Inclusivity in Church of Christ Congregations." An Executive Summary of the Research Project conducted by Stephen Johnson, D.Min., Th.D. and Lynette Sharp Penya, Ph.D. October 2010. http://halfthe-church.files.wordpress.com/2010/10/executive-summary1.pdf.

The "Gender-Inclusive" Movement
Among Churches of Christ

only 40.9% had women serving as "deacons," they noted that "some respondents indicated their congregations use the formal title 'Ministry Leader' for women instead of 'Deacon'" (2). They found 34.1% used women for what they called "Ministry Leaders" (6). Although as of October 2010 there were no congregations that had appointed women as elders, they reported that "a few congregations noted women have been nominated as elders in their congregations in the past but have not yet been chosen for that position" (2). We saw in the first chapter that one of the criteria Clarkson uses to identify "Gender-Inclusive" churches is the question: "Do women serve in leadership positions such as pulpit minister, worship leader, deacon, and ELDER?" (emphasis mine).[2] This would suggest to us that we can assume it is only a matter of time before advocates of the "gender-inclusive" movement achieve this objective as well.

Should We Appoint Women Elders and Deacons?

It is interesting that Johnson and Penya's research indicated more reservation among these congregations to appoint women elders than there was to appoint women deacons. From a biblical standpoint the issue is much the same. A clear biblical qualification demanded of both leaders is that they must be **"the husband of one wife"** (1 Tim. 3:2; cf. 3:12). Even so, it is often falsely asserted that there were female deacons in the New Testament church.

This assertion stems largely from the fact by the fourth century the Eastern churches had established an office for women deacons, but this proves nothing about New Testament practice. West-

---

[2] January 11, 2012 update, http://www.clarksons.org/spiritleads/gender_inclusive_churches.htm.

The "Gender-Inclusive" Movement
Among Churches of Christ

ern churches had established the office of "pope" by the fourth century, but it was just as unscriptural. The earliest evidence advocates can appeal to is a second century letter written by the pagan governor Pliny to the Roman emperor Trajan regarding the torture of two Christian women whom he says were called "*ministrae*," the feminine form of the Latin equivalent of

> The evidence does not prove that there were female deacons in the early history of the church.

the Greek word *diakonos* (διάκονος) from which the word "deacon" is translated (*Letters* 10.96.8). Unfortunately, many English translations of this text render *ministrae* "deaconesses," but that assumes more than is warranted by the text itself, and reads the later practice into the earlier text. The fact is that the Latin word *minister* like the Greek *diakonos* can have a specific or generic meaning in reference to one who is simply a "servant."

Were There Women Deacons in the New Testament Church?

I know of a liberal congregation that decided some time ago that if they appointed women "deacons" too many people would object. To avoid controversy they essentially dissolved the role of deacons and appointed male and female "ministers" instead. It is true that the Greek word *diakonos* means simply "servant," and properly a *minister* is a servant. Even so, we must recognize that there is something wrong with our commitment to follow the pattern of Scripture if are willing to eliminate a biblical role of organization in the local church, but have no problem with creating a new one?

We could call "deacons" by any number of names that accurately translate the Greek word *diakonos* including servant, minister, or even attendant (see Strong's Greek 1249). This would not, however, change the fact that very specific qualifications have been set for these appointed leaders within a local church. The Holy Spirit commands, **"Let deacons be the husbands of one wife, ruling their children and their own houses well"** (1 Tim. 3:12). In spite of what advocates of "same-sex marriage" say, a woman cannot be *the husband of one wife*! That makes it clear that a woman cannot be a servant of the church in the same sense outlined in these qualifications.

Critics point out properly that the word *gunē* (γυνή), translated "wife," in the Greek is the same word that means simply "woman." So they argue that what Paul was addressing is polygamy—that is, that a deacon must be a "one woman man." We would agree that this too is inferred in the command, but it goes too far to try and apply this to the previous verse. "Gender-inclusive" advocates argue that 1 Timothy 3:11, rather than describing qualifications of the "wives" of elders and deacons, instead offers qualifications for "women" who serve as deacons. The problem with this interpretation is the presence of the adverb **"likewise"**—*hōsau-*

> The context indicates that 1 Timothy 3:11 concerns wives of male leaders, not female deacons.

tōs (ὡσαύτως) at the beginning of verse eleven. It is translated **"even so"** (KJV), **"in like manner"** (ASV), **"in the same way"** (NIV), and most frequently **"likewise"** (RSV, NASB, NKJV, ESV). It indicates a comparison or contrast. The same word is used in verse eight when Paul shifts from talking about elders to list qualifications for deacons. So what is the contrast or comparison? Paul can't be talking about the same group of people (i.e. deacons) because in the next verse he says, **"Let deacons be the husbands of one wife."** He was talking about deacons before verse eleven and returns to the same subject in verse twelve. So who are the "women" of verse eleven? Certainly all women are to be "reverent, not slanderers, temperate, faithful in all things," but contextually we must conclude that the "women" of verse eleven are the "wives" of whom both deacons (3:12) and elders (3:2), are to have only "one." If verse eleven was talking about women deacons, we would expect verse twelve to add the phrase "or the wife of one husband"—a qualification given later of widows supported by the church (cf. 1 Tim. 5:9). The text doesn't add this! The only way we could argue that the women of verse eleven are female deacons (or elders) is if we argued that they too must be **"husbands of one wife"**—a condition clearly forbidden by the biblical teaching regarding homosexuality (Rom. 1:26-27).

What About Phoebe?

In Romans 16:1 a woman is mentioned by the name of Phoebe. Most translations properly refer to her as a **"servant of the church in Cenchrea."** The word translated "servant" in this text is the feminine form of the word translated "deacon" in some other places. Several of the modern translations have a footnote attached to this word reading—**"Or, deaconess"** (ASV, NIV). The Revised Standard actually uses the word **"deaconess"** in the text and the New Revised Standard calls her **"a deacon."** We must note that the word *diakonos* can be used in a generic sense of servants, and in a specific sense of the appointed servants in a local church. This is seen in the fact that the King James version translated it three times "deacon," twenty times "minister," and seven times simply "servant" (7). Most often when it was used in the New Testament it was not referring to the appointed, qualified servants of the local church but to servants in general. This is especially clear in Galatians 2:17 where it refers to Christ. He was a servant, but not a "deacon" of a local church. Why would we assume anything different about Phoebe? She was a servant of the church in Cenchrea, but she was not a "deacon" because she was not (and could not lawfully have been)— **"the husband of one wife."**

"Why Should this Matter to Me?"

When considering issues of controversy or apostasy it is very easy to say to ourselves, "That could never happen here—that's someone else's problem." Sadly, in far too many cases potential problems ignored are problems waiting to explode.

Over a decade ago I visited a sound congregation of Christians in the Midwest. This congregation had begun to conduct their Sunday evening services like a Bible class, in which women made comments from the pew, read Scriptures, and discussed issues that were being taught by a male teacher. The problem was that they made no indication on their sign or in their announcements that there was anything different about their Bible class, and when they assembled "as a church." To the visitor it simply appeared as if women were speaking "in church." I voiced concerns about it at the time, but hoped that it was just a lack of appropriate communication and a lack proper caution. Sadly, that congregation is no longer in existence and some of its former members now worship with a "gender-inclusive" liberal congregation in the same town.

One of its former members recently spoke in Houston at the CBE ("Christians for Biblical Equality") conference. Explaining

The "Gender-Inclusive" Movement
Among Churches of Christ

the evolution of her change in thinking, she cited a class she sat in 20 years ago in an "extremely conservative church" when she noticed for the first time that "women were prophesying and praying at the church in Corinth." I assume she was talking about 1 Corinthians 11:4-5 where Paul

Dangerous tendencies ignored are problems waiting to explode.

discussed the head covering that women were to wear when praying or prophesying. She explained that she asked the teacher about it, and he said, "the women MUST have been doing this in private in their own homes" (emphasis hers). This didn't satisfy her, leading her to conclude, "this was ridiculous and I knew it! Where else had they ever seen mention of someone prophesying that they would say that about? It goes against the very meaning of the word!"[3]

How I wish I could have been in that class 20 years ago! We could have talked about Miriam, who was identified as a **"prophetess"** (Exod. 15:20) but is never recorded as having spoken before the formal assembly of Israel. In fact, when she and Aaron questioned Moses' authority, she was given leprosy for seven days as a punishment (Num. 12:1-16). We could have talked about Deborah, the **"prophetess"** and judge (Judg. 4:4). She too, was never said to have addressed the assembly of Israel, but sat under a palm tree between Ramah and Bethel and the Israelites came to her for judgment (Judg. 4:5). We could have talked about Huldah, the prophetess who gave the frightening prophecy in the days of Josiah that Judah would fall. She did not address the assembly—the priest Hilkiah came to her home in the section of Jerusalem called

---

[3] http://www.cbehouston.org/Pages/Marilyn.aspx.

The "Gender-Inclusive" Movement
Among Churches of Christ

"the Second Quarter" to hear this prophecy (2 Kings 22:14-20; 2 Chron. 34:22-28). Even, Anna, the prophetess who proclaimed the identity of Jesus, did so in the temple courts—not in a synagogue or a formal assembly of Israel (Luke 2:36-38). There is nothing in the word "prophesy" that demands that the prophecy be revealed in the assembly of the church.

In the next chapter we will draw our study to a close by addressing some final considerations that must be answered in dealing with this very serious and alarming issue.

Study Questions

1. Scripturally is it any less a violation of Scripture to appoint women deacons than it is to appoint women elders? Why would churches do one and resist the other?
2. To whom is the word *diakonos* applied in Galatians 2:17? Was this person a "deacon" in a local church?
3. From the context, how can we know that 1 Timothy 3:11 is not listing qualifications for female deacons?

Final Considerations

We end our study of the "Gender-Inclusive" movement among churches of Christ with a few important final questions and considerations.

Can a Woman Speak in Bible Class?

We have seen in our study that the restrictions regarding women speaking and teaching identify very specific contexts in which particular prohibitions apply. The Bible authorizes women to speak in discussions of the Bible in situations outside of the church assembly (Acts 18:24-26). We have also seen that the Bible teaches that in such situations a woman is not to exercise authority over a man and is to maintain a quiet disposition (1 Tim. 2:11-12). This makes it clear that in Bible classes of God's people that are not understood to involve a congregation assembled as a church, whether at a congregation's meeting house or somewhere else, a woman is authorized to speak. It is when the church is assembled "in the church" that a woman is forbidden to speak at all (1 Cor. 14:34-35). We should note, that some differentiation must be made. It is not about *worship* vs. *Bible class*—it is about whether we are "in the church" vs. a gathering for a different purpose. We would do

> The Bible authorizes women to speak in discussions of the Bible outside of the church assembly.

well in our announcements or other communication to make it clear when "we are now assembled as a church."

What about Singing?

A fundamental principle of biblical interpretation is that any command of Scripture carries with it all that is necessary to obey that command. No command of Scripture countermands another command. In this issue it is clear that a woman is commanded to absolute silence when the local church is assembled (1 Cor. 14:34-35), however, the silence that is commanded "in the church" does not countermand the charge all Christians are given to worship by **"singing and making melody in your hearts to the Lord"** (Eph. 5:19b). In this text in Ephesians Paul describes this activity as something that involves "speaking to one another in psalms and hymns and spiritual songs" (Eph. 5:19a). Paul's word translated "speaking" is actually a form of the same Greek word *laleō* (λαλέω), he used in 1 Corinthians 14:34-35. Is this a contradiction? No. Obviously, to sing to each other is "speaking" or "teaching" (Col. 3:16) in a sense, but it involves a collective action that is different from one person in a normal voice "speaking" or "teaching." In 1 Corinthians 14:34-35 Paul is not talking about the collective musical *speaking*. In 1 Timothy 2:11-12 Paul is not talking about collective musical *teaching* that can occur when we sing to one another. The Holy Spirit leads Paul to prohibit individual speaking or teaching in a normal voice.

> No command of Scripture countermands another command.

The same is true of confession. If a woman accepts the gospel invitation and comes forward when the church is assembled to obey the gospel, must she "be silent" regarding her confession of faith in Christ? All human beings are commanded to confess faith in Jesus "before men" (Matt. 10:32-33). For this limited activity and specific purpose Scripture clearly authorizes a woman to speak in or out of the assembly of the church in her confession of Christ. This does not, however, change the fact that the general regulation taught in Scripture restricts a woman from speaking in other cases when the church is assembled.

When Does a Boy Become a Man?

As long as I have been preaching a quiet question rumbles in the background from time to time. A godly woman who devotes herself to teaching young children teaches them diligently about matters from Bible history to the plan of salvation. Then one day, the fruit of her labors is realized and a young boy in her class obeys the gospel. *Can a woman teach a class over a baptized young boy?* This is much like the question "when is the age of accountability?" The Bible has not given a specific answer to either of these questions, but caution, discretion, and humility must be demonstrated by all involved in such matters if we are to follow the standard of God's word. Most elderships conclude *since we are not told when a boy comes to be considered a man, in order to avoid the violation of 1 Timothy 2:11, women are not allowed to teach boys who have been baptized boys.*

If we are not careful emotion can easily cloud this issue. The godly woman who taught this young boy might be tempted to feel hurt, thinking "I taught him—I know more than he does. Now you are saying I can no longer teach him?" The issue is obedi-

The "Gender-Inclusive" Movement
Among Churches of Christ

ence to biblical teaching. It is never about *who knows more*. Thanks be to God for the scores of knowledgeable Christian women who have motivated our young people to faith. On the other hand, the young boy might be tempted to think, "I'm a man now—you can't teach me anything!" That is arrogance and a misguided understanding of the issue! Certainly the manner of the teaching may change but it is fool-hearty to think that there is nothing that one can learn from older sisters in the faith. Roles may change, but maturity and spiritual knowledge must always be respected.

In this and other difficult questions, I fear that the mocking attitude of the "gender-inclusive" movement misses the serious issues that underlie this matter. *How may we follow God's word in all things?* When difficult questions arise, will we reject the biblical teachings that lead to such difficult questions or will we do our best to humbly obey them? That is the issue.

What about Non-speaking Acts of Public Worship?

After offering his understanding on 1 Corinthians 14:34-35, Edward Fudge concludes that even "its most literalistic interpretation would still not prevent women as well as men from acting as ushers, serving the Lord's Supper, or taking up the offering, to name just a few silent areas where women often are not permitted to serve" ("Women 'Be Silent' in Church (1)").[1] This raises some points worthy of consideration. We would agree that neither 1 Corinthians 14:34-35 or 1 Timothy 2:11-12 necessarily prohibit women from serving in some of these activities which are essentially authorized expedients by which commanded activities are carried out. However, we must also recognize that some of these tasks constitute the

---

[1] http://www.wherethespiritleads.org/spiritleads/Women%20Be%20Silent.htm.

The "Gender-Inclusive" Movement
Among Churches of Christ

initial activities that usher young men into more public acts of leadership in worship within the church. A young Christian boy first learns how to pass the plate so no one is missed, and then he is given the responsibility to thank the Lord for the elements of the Lord's Supper. How easy, in a world already pushing young women to reject male authority, will it be to let them take the *first steps*, but then deny them the *next steps?* This may lay an unnecessary stumbling-block before our sisters in Christ.

A more serious consideration needs to be addressed. In the years that I have been preaching, an interesting tendency is seen from time to time. Occasionally, both men and women who are inactive in areas of work within the church, sometimes want to assert themselves into very public functions when they have not previously demonstrated diligence in other tasks. When my wife and I were recently talking about whether it would be appropriate for women to perform some roles of public worship that do not involve

> Will it be easy for us to deny women the next steps if we introduce them to the first steps?

speaking or leading over a man, she raised a very good point. She noted that there are more than enough things that fall within the authority of Scripture that women who wish to can choose to carry out, without feeling the necessity to hand out visitor's cards, pass the communion plate, etc. Paul mentions some of these in the qualifications for widows supported by the church. A widow may be supported only if she is **"well reported for good works: if she has brought up children, if she has lodged strangers, if she has washed the saints' feet, if she has relieved the afflict-**

The "Gender-Inclusive" Movement
Among Churches of Christ

ed, if she has diligently followed every good work" (1 Tim. 5:10). These things don't necessarily involve any public activities of worship within the church assembly, but they are indispensable to the spiritual health of a congregation.

Have we allowed our world's estimation of the worth of these things to make us think they are less valuable? Are we tempted to aspire to things in the "public eye" to the neglect of these essential quiet acts of service? We might do well to remember that although it was men who stood up to teach on the Day of Pentecost (Acts 2:14), it was a group of faithful women that provided for Jesus **"from their own substance"** (Luke 8:3), who were said to have **"followed Jesus from Galilee, ministering to Him"** (Matt. 27:55). When the apostles ran away, women came to the tomb to anoint His dead body (Mark 16:1), and Jesus first appeared to women (Mark 16:9)—but there is no record of a woman speaking or leading activities of public worship.

What Is the Standard?

The woman I mentioned in the previous chapter who once worshipped with a sound congregation and now advocates the "gender-inclusive" view, told listeners at the Houston conference of the CBE International ("Christians for Biblical Equality") that she would have changed her view earlier if she had not ignored the "the urgings of the Spirit."[2] This same mindset is reflected in the website Clarkson hosts listing churches considered "Gender-Inclusive." It is not called *What Does the Bible Say?*—but *Where the Spirit Leads*. This betrays a broader problem that complicates this whole issue. It is a problem that rests at the heart of the diffi-

---

[2] http://www.cbehouston.org/Pages/Marilyn.aspx.

The "Gender-Inclusive" Movement
Among Churches of Christ

culty we face with the denominational world as a whole when it comes to calling people to unity in Christ. If we will accept the Bible as the inspired revelation of the Holy Spirit and agree to follow where it leads and restrain ourselves where it has not spoken (or where it restricts our behavior) we can achieve unity. If each us claims that the Holy Spirit leads us in directions different from one another, and contrary to the revelation He has previously set forth, unity is impossible. We would do well to remember what the Holy Spirit has previously told us—**"God is not the author of confusion but of peace"** (1 Cor. 14:33).

Study Questions

1. What are some problems with concluding that the church is assembled "as a church" when it is broken up into Bible classes?
2. What are things that are different about "speaking to one another" in song, and the prohibition of 1 Corinthians 14:34-35?
3. What are some works that are essential to the health of a congregation a woman can do without violation of any Scripture?

Appendix: The Assembly and the Work of the Church —A Clarification

When I first wrote on the rise of the so-called "Gender-Inclusive" Movement in our church bulletin a question came up that required clarification. In discussing the distinction that exists between when the church assembles **"as a church"** (1 Cor. 11:18) and when some members of the congregation assemble for a Bible class, I gave one brother the impression I was saying that a Bible class was not a part of the work of the church. At that time I offered a few points that helped to clarify this matter which I now offer for the reader to consider.

Bible Classes are a Work of the Church

Paul taught Timothy that the church is the **"pillar and ground of the truth"** (1 Tim. 3:15). He taught the Ephesians that different workers within the church have been set in place **"for the equipping of the saints for the work of ministry, for the edifying of the body of Christ"** (Eph. 4:12, NKJV). It is well within the authorized work of the church for elders to appoint teachers for different classes, whether divided by age or subject matter, and oversee and fund the teaching efforts they carry out. This could be done at the place where the church assembles, or in other locations. This fact, however, demonstrates one of the points addressed in the previous chapters—not every work of the church is done by the congregation as a whole, or when the church is assembled—"as a church."

Works of the Church that *Do Not* Involve the Whole Congregation

Let's note a couple of examples where Scripture shows works of the church being carried out without the whole church being assembled together. In Acts 20:17-38 Paul returned to the region of Ephesus where he had worked for two years (Acts 19:10). Because of the danger he faced in Ephesus, he called the elders of the church in Ephesus to meet him in the nearby city of Miletus. Did this concern the work of the church in Ephesus? Absolutely! (See Acts 20:28.) Did it involve every member of the that congregation? No. Were Paul and the elders assembled "as a church"? No. Where I preach, every Sunday afternoon the elders follow a similar procedure. We assemble at five o'clock for our weekly *elders' meeting.* Usually it is just the elders. Is this something that is a work of the church? Absolutely. That is the entire focus of the meeting. However, could we say that the elders are meeting "as a church" or "in the church"? No.

> Elders' meetings are an example of a work of the church that does not involve the church assembled.

Let's consider another example. In Acts chapter six, when a need arose for the church to supply food to the widows of the congregation in Jerusalem, was that considered an authorized work of the church? Yes, but seven men were appointed to address this need focused on a smaller part of the congregation as a whole (Acts 6:3-5). This was not carried out by the church as a whole.

The "Gender-Inclusive" Movement
Among Churches of Christ

They were not "in church" (i.e., in the assembly) or assembled together "as a church" when it was done. This shows us that it is possible to engage in a *work* of the church without the church being assembled as a whole or when meeting "as a church."

Bible Classes and Assemblies of the Church

In the previous chapters we considered carefully the restrictions and context that regulate when and how women may and may not speak and teach. We demonstrated that Scripture shows us that you can have a study outside of the assembly of the church in which a woman may speak with men about spiritual matters (Acts 18:24-26), although she may not teach over a man (1 Tim. 2:11-12). We found that Paul commands that a woman must be silent within the assembly of the church (1 Cor. 14:34-35), but the question is, *does a Bible class constitute the church assembled "as a church"?* Not necessarily. Where I preach, when we have classes there are generally no times when all of the members of the church are assembled all together. Some are teaching children. Some are teaching teenagers. Recently, we began an additional adult class on Wednesday night. When it meets some adults are in a separate class. In these nine different classes are we ever actually "in the church" (i.e., in the assembly) or assembled "as a church"? No. If so, women would have to be silent. Are these nine separate assemblies of the church? No. If so, we have nine churches! Now, does this mean that these nine classes are not part of the work of the church? No. Just like the example in Acts chapter six, different

> **Not all Bible classes involve the whole church assembled "as a church."**

members of the church have been appointed to carry out a specific work of the church directed towards a smaller segment of the congregation.

What if the whole church assembled for a Bible class. If the stated purpose of that assembly was to "come together as a church" then women would have to be silent. On the other hand, if a distinction was made and the stated purpose of the assembly was not to assemble "as a church," even though every member of the local congregation might be present it would not necessar-

> It is possible for every member of a church to be together and yet not be "in the church."

ily be an assembly" of the church, or "in the church." This is where it often becomes complicated to us. We struggle with the question, *how could every member be present and it not constitute the church?* Let's think of it this way—imagine a congregation of ten members. These ten members are from three families. Family A has five members. Family B has three members. Family C has two members. Are they assembled "as a church" any time all ten people are together? Are they "in the church" if they go out to eat together, or go shopping, or camping together? No. If they chose to study a topic with all three families in their home, would they be "in the church"? Not necessarily. Are they "in the church" whenever they all enter the place where they assemble? Not necessarily. If so, the minute they are in sight of each other, women would have to be silent. It is possible then, for every member of a local congregation to be together without being assem-

The "Gender-Inclusive" Movement
Among Churches of Christ

bled "as a church." What determines this distinction? The stated purpose of the assembly.

Individual versus Church Responsibilities

One final point is appropriate in this consideration. We have noted instances in which the work of the church does not demand that the entire church be assembled. Are there ever times when the responsibilities of the individual and the church differ? Absolutely! As a husband and father I am to provide for my family (1 Tim. 5:8). Is the church to provide for my family? The church may relieve a need (Acts 11:29), but it is not to be burdened with providing for them in general (1 Tim. 5:16). Here we see an overlap, and a limitation. The same is true in spiritual training. As a father I am to bring up my children **"in the training and admonition of the Lord"** (Eph. 6:4). The church is also to *equip* the saints (Eph. 4:12). Can I surrender to the church my responsibility? No. Is the church usurping my role when it helps in this? No. I have an individual responsibility, and the church has a collective responsibility.

Are there responsibilities that the church does not share with the individual? Yes. A husband and wife have responsibilities to each other that involve no one outside of that relationship (1 Cor. 7:3-5). We understand in this case that the church cannot involve itself in that responsibility, except to the degree that it must teach about marriage and its biblical regulation. There are many other good works that the individual may engage in that the church has no right to involve itself in. For example, we have the account that Christians in Jerusalem ate together with one another in their homes (Acts 2:46), but we are also told that this was not to be

The "Gender-Inclusive" Movement
Among Churches of Christ

done "as a church" (1 Cor. 11:17-34). A sound church does not eat together "as a church" but it is not uncommon for individuals who are a part of a sound church to get together in a home, a restaurant, or even at a private facility secured with individual funds. I know of a situation where some of the ladies of a congregation had a study

There are responsibilities the church and the individual share and those which they do not.

with a guest speaker. It was not a work of the church—it was all done by individuals. It involved some singing and study (which are works of the church) but it also involved eating together (which is not a work of the church). By handling it as an individual effort, there was no conflict.

The problem is that in much of the world, as modern churches have expanded the work of the church to involve everything from business ventures, to medical and psychological activities, social functions, and entertainment, they have confused the clear teaching of Scripture, and acted without divine authority. We must understand and respect the work of the church as God has established it and demonstrated it in Scripture. We must fulfill the responsibilities we have as individuals whether they overlap with the work of the church or not. We must, however, do all that we can to shun the influence of our society to expand the work of the church beyond what Scripture has authorized.

Scripture Index

The "Gender-Inclusive" Movement
Among Churches of Christ

General Index

The "Gender-Inclusive" Movement
Among Churches of Christ

www.ingramcontent.com/pod-product-compliance
Lightning Source LLC
Chambersburg PA
CBHW060540030426
42337CB00021B/4361